W9-AOP-173

ROCKFORD PUBLIC LIBRARY
3 1112 014555517 7

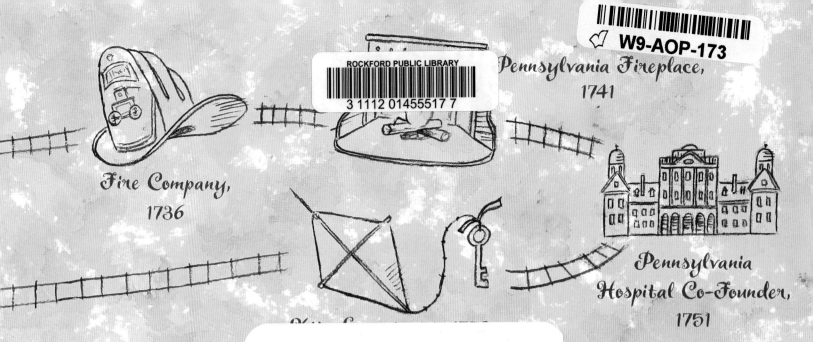

Fire Company,
1736

Pennsylvania Fireplace,
1741

Pennsylvania
Hospital Co-Founder,
1751

Library Chair,
1761

...monica, circa 1762

Declaration of
Independence, 1776

Charted
the Gulf Stream,
1768–1785

U.S. Constitution,
1787

E BARRETTA, G
Barretta, Gene.
Now & Ben :
the modern inventions of
Benjamin Franklin /

032306

WITHDRAWN

ROCKFORD PUBLIC LIBRARY
Rockford, Illinois
www.rockfordpubliclibrary.org
815-965-9511

For my son, Benjamin, who reminds
me to fill each day with wonder
and discovery—Dr. Franklin would
be proud of you —Love, Daddy

Special thanks to Neil Di Sabato,
Roy Goodman, Neil Ronk, Adam Potkay,
Bill Ochester, and Ralph Archbold

Henry Holt and Company, LLC, *Publishers since 1866*
175 Fifth Avenue, New York, New York 10010 [www.henryholtchildrensbooks.com]

Henry Holt® is a registered trademark of Henry Holt and Company, LLC. Copyright © 2006 by Gene Barretta.
All rights reserved. Distributed in Canada by H. B. Fenn and Company Ltd.

Library of Congress Cataloging-in-Publication Data
Barretta, Gene.
Now & Ben : the modern inventions of Benjamin Franklin / by Gene Barretta.—1st ed.
   p.   cm.
ISBN-13: 978-0-8050-7917-3 / ISBN-10: 0-8050-7917-3
1. Franklin, Benjamin, 1706–1790. 2. Inventions—United States—History—Juvenile literature. 3. Inventors—
United States—Juvenile literature. I. Title: Now and Ben. II. Title: Modern inventions of Benjamin Franklin. III. Title.
T48.B27 2006   609'.2—dc22   2005012491

First Edition—2006 / Designed by Laurent Linn and Amy Manzo Toth
The artist used watercolor on paper to create the illustrations for this book.
Printed in China. 10 9 8 7 6 5 4 3 2 1

Now & Ben

The Modern Inventions of Benjamin Franklin

GENE BARRETTA

Henry Holt and Company
New York

ROCKFORD PUBLIC LIBRARY

SON
FRANCIS

SON
WILLIAM

DAUGHTER
SALLY

WIFE

DEBORAH

Now and then, we think about Ben.
Dr. Benjamin Franklin, to be precise.
And we think about his many inventions—
inventions he originated more than two hundred years ago.

It was as if Ben could see into the future.
Almost everything he created is still around today.
For instance . . .

Now... our newspapers are filled with illustrations.

Ben . . . was the first to print a political cartoon in America. The cartoon encouraged the American colonies to join together or die like the disconnected snake.

Now... bifocals are very common. Bifocals combine two sets of lenses into one pair of glasses. The bottom lens helps see near, and the top lens helps see far.

SEE FAR

SEE NEAR

Ben... originally designed bifocals for himself after he grew tired of switching between two pairs of glasses.

SEE FAR

SEE NEAR

Now... our world relies on electricity. In the eighteenth century, many people still believed that lightning was an act of anger and punishment from God.

Ben ... was one of the scientists who discovered the true nature of electricity and how to use it. He learned that lightning is electricity when he attached a small metal wire to the top of a kite and gathered electricity from a storm cloud.

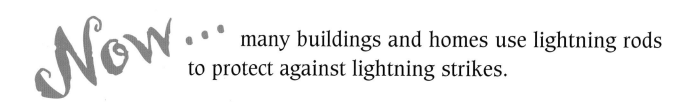

Now... many buildings and homes use lightning rods to protect against lightning strikes.

Ben... invented the lightning rod and was the first to use it. The pointed iron rod acts like a magnet and grabs an approaching lightning bolt from the sky before it can strike the rooftop. The electricity then travels safely down a long wire into the ground. It prevents fires and keeps dangerous amounts of electricity away from the house.

Now ...

this gadget goes by many names, such as the Grabber. Everyone has seen one—it's the long stick that helps grab items from out-of-reach places.

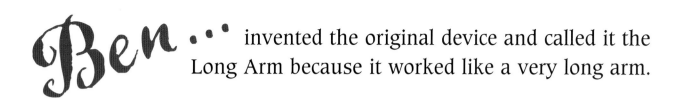

Ben... invented the original device and called it the Long Arm because it worked like a very long arm.

Now... swimmers and divers use flippers to move faster through the water. →

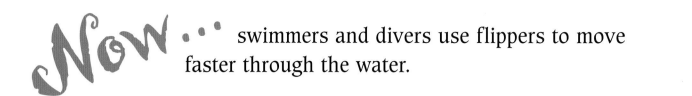

Now... ships travel across the Gulf Stream to take advantage of the faster current. →

Now... we understand and accept the benefits of vitamin C. →

Ben... invented things even when he was a boy. He was an avid swimmer and built wooden flippers for both his hands and feet.

Ben... measured, charted, and publicized the Gulf Stream during his eight voyages across the Atlantic Ocean.

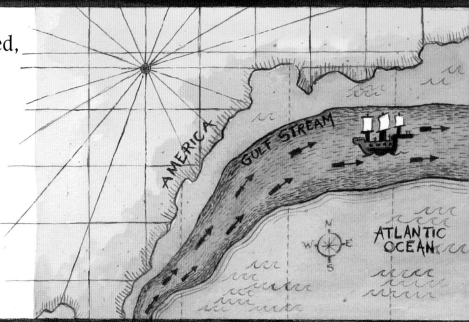

Ben... was an early promoter of eating citrus fruits to help prevent a disease called scurvy.

Ben... invented the glass armonica. He was able to create music by simply touching his wet fingers to a row of spinning glass bowls. Mozart and Beethoven were so moved by the sounds that they composed for the instrument.

TUNED GLASS BOWLS TURN ON A ROD

WHEEL TURNS THE GLASS BOWLS →

TUNED GLASS BOWLS

FOOT PEDAL MAKES THE WHEEL TURN →

ARMONICA

Today, glass armonicas are very rare. You are more likely to find one in a museum than in a music store.

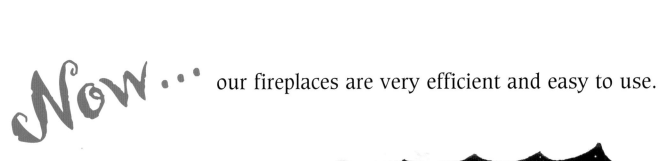

Now... our fireplaces are very efficient and easy to use.

Ben ... improved on the primitive fireplaces of his day when he designed the Pennsylvania Fireplace, later renamed the Franklin stove. He built it with iron to contain the heat from a fire long after the logs were burned. It also sat away from the wall to heat the room more evenly.

The smoke ventilation was not perfect, but later inventors improved it. Before Ben's fireplace, indoor smoke could be suffocating.

Now… chairs come in all shapes and sizes. →

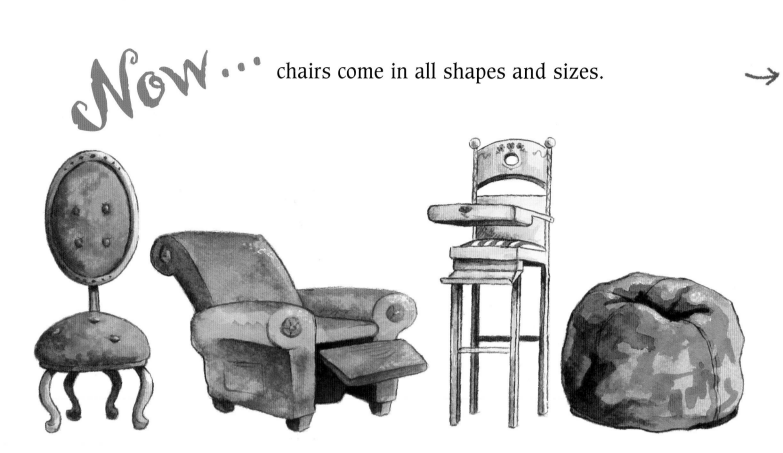

Now… everyone has seen a rocking chair, but not many have seen Dr. Franklin's rocking chairs. →

Ben ... designed two chairs that are still very useful.

The writing chair combined a desk and chair into one.

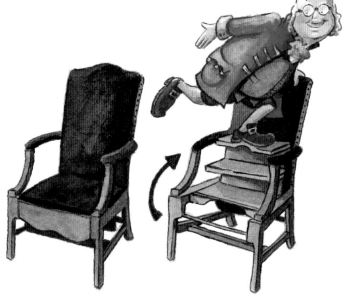

The library chair was a combination chair and stepladder.

Ben ... invented one rocking chair with a fan on top and one that churned butter.

$\mathcal{N}ow \ldots$ every year, we observe daylight saving time, which means we set our clocks ahead one hour in the springtime. As a result, it stays darker longer in the morning when most people are sleeping and stays light longer at the end of the day so we can save more energy. In the fall, we return the clocks to standard time.

Ben... suggested this idea in one of his essays as a way to save money by burning fewer candles. Farmers could also gain more work time in the evening. Daylight saving time was not officially practiced until World War I, more than a hundred years later.

As for clocks . . .
Ben designed the first clock with a second hand.

Now... every automobile has an odometer to measure the distance it travels.

MILEAGE

Ben... invented the odometer when he was postmaster general so he could measure his postal routes.

Now... almost every large community includes a library, a hospital, a post office, a fire department, and a sanitation department.

Ben... lived in a city that had none of these establishments, so he helped organize the first of each.

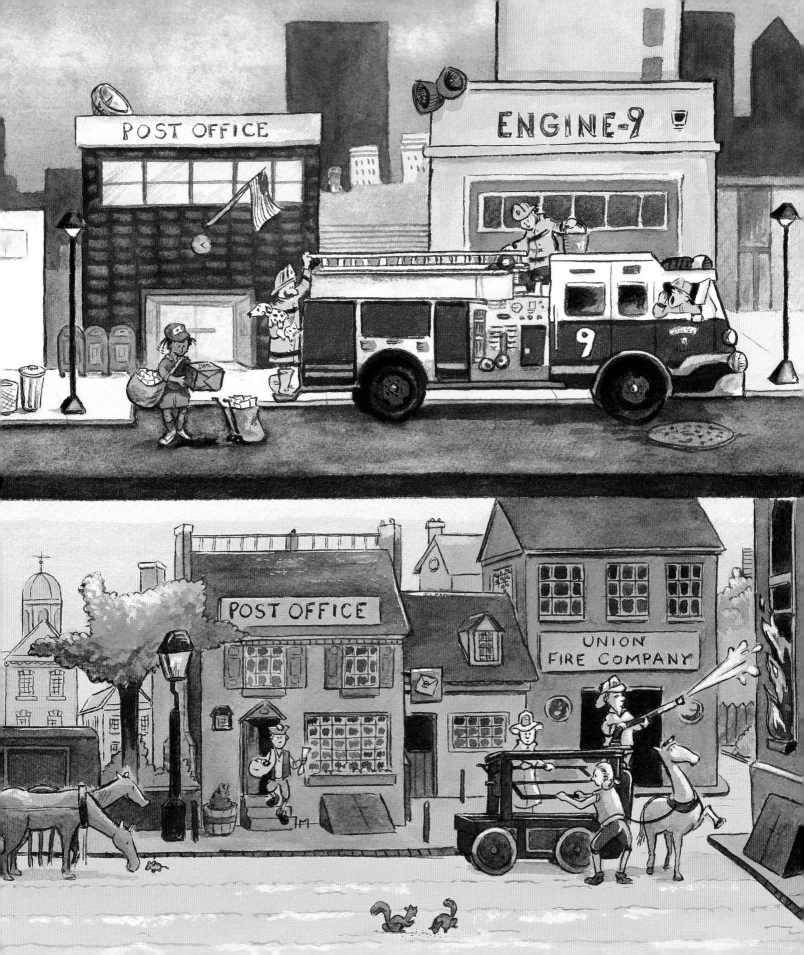

Now... and then, we owe thanks to Ben for his important inventions. But many would agree that his greatest accomplishments came in the form of documents—documents that helped shape the world.

$\mathcal{B}en\ldots$ had a pivotal role in developing America's Constitution, the Treaty of Alliance with France, the Treaty of Peace with England, and the Declaration of Independence.

It's remarkable that one man could achieve so much in a lifetime. He has certainly helped to form the modern world. . . .

Will his contributions help to form the future?

Swim Fins, 1717

Public Library in America, 1731

Sanitation Department, circa 1736

Odometer, 1753

Home Delivery Postal Service, 1753

Lightning Rod, 1752

Political Cartoon in America, 1754

Treaty of Alliance (with France), 1778

Treaty of Peace (with England), 1783

Bifocals, 1784

Daylight Saving Time, 1784